7 SECRETS NOBODY TOLD YOU

ABOUT SUCCESSFUL CAREER

Angammai Monika

Chennai • Bangalore

CLEVER FOX PUBLISHING
Chennai, India

Published by CLEVER FOX PUBLISHING 2023
Copyright © Angammai Monika 2023

All Rights Reserved.
ISBN: 978-93-56482-98-2

This book has been published with all reasonable efforts taken to make the material error-free after the consent of the author. No part of this book shall be used, reproduced in any manner whatsoever without written permission from the author, except in the case of brief quotations embodied in critical articles and reviews.

The Author of this book is solely responsible and liable for its content including but not limited to the views, representations, descriptions, statements, information, opinions and references ["Content"]. The Content of this book shall not constitute or be construed or deemed to reflect the opinion or expression of the Publisher or Editor. Neither the Publisher nor Editor endorse or approve the Content of this book or guarantee the reliability, accuracy or completeness of the Content published herein and do not make any representations or warranties of any kind, express or implied, including but not limited to the implied warranties of merchantability, fitness for a particular purpose. The Publisher and Editor shall not be liable whatsoever for any errors, omissions, whether such errors or omissions result from negligence, accident, or any other cause or claims for loss or damages of any kind, including without limitation, indirect or consequential loss or damage arising out of use, inability to use, or about the reliability, accuracy or sufficiency of the information contained in this book.

DEDICATION

I dedicate this book to my wonderful parents Mrs.N.Santhanalakshmi (Retired Govt. Teacher) & Mr.SP.M.Nagappan (Retired Licensing Manager).

Dear mom & dad, you are my best friends. You accept me for everything I am and love me unconditionally. You are the people who have made me the woman that I am today. Your valuable advice has guided me to face challenging situations.

I Love you, mom & dad.

Success is the progressive realization of a worthy goal or ideal.
— ***Earl Nightingale***

TABLE OF CONTENTS

Preface .... *vi*
About the Author .... *viii*

1. The Real Meaning of Success 1

2. Secret No.1 Set a Definite Goal 4

3. Secret No. 2 Breaking Out of Conformity 19

4. Secret No.3 Become Perseverant 24

5. Secret No.4 Embrace Failure 29

6. Secret No.5 Stop Worrying 36

7. Secret No.6 Beat Your Smartphone Addiction 43

8. Secret No.7 The Power of Asking For Help 53

Client Testimonials *58*
Epilogue *64*
Summary *65*
Acknowledgement *66*

PREFACE

"Which career has higher possibilities of making someone successful"?

It is the most frequently asked question throughout my career coaching journey. People across the globe, from students to professionals have asked this question in different ways, which made me choose this topic for my first book.

The reality is that no career comes with a success tag. Instead of making the choice purely based on the popularity of a career, I highly recommend you to choose a career that is in alignment with your passion, core personality, strengths, interest & skills which in turn will help you build a successful career.

Through my book, I intend to share my years of experience & hours of research to guide people, especially students & young professionals to design their dream careers & in turn enjoy their lives to the fullest.

Most often anyone who wishes to write a book starts with 50 pages & develops it to 1000 pages. But I am doing it

Preface

reverse from 1000 to 50 pages. Just to make it as easy & simple as possible, so that none of my friends finds time as a constraint for reading the book. By investing just 20 min of your time you can save 20 years of your career.

ABOUT THE AUTHOR

Angammai Monika is a Transformational Career Coach, Top Career Counsellor, Mentor & Founder of Ebullient Career Counselling. She is a certified career counsellor by IAAP (International Association Of Applied Psychology, APCDA (Asia Pacific Career Development Association), ACCPH (Accredited Counsellors, Coaches, Psychotherapists & Hypnotherapists). Pursuing PCC Program from ICF (International Coaching Federation).

She has a work experience of 16 years in 10 different domains & been associated with renowned organizations like Randstad, IBM, American Express, Supreme Industries & Greenpeace.

Through this wide range of experience, she has successfully counselled, coached & mentored 1000+ students & professionals across India & abroad. She has catered her services to students starting from 8th grade to professionals with 30+ years of experience.

Her Vision is to see a world where everyone is doing a job that they love.

About the Author

Her Mission is to unleash the true potential of 1 million people to do a job that they are passionate about through career coaching.

She enjoys reading self-development books, spending time with family & traveling.

Clients have shared their high level of satisfaction with 5-star ratings & heartfelt messages on the website & google review page. Link mentioned below.

https://ebullient.edumilestones.com

https://g.co/kgs/J5ZoAs

Can be reached @

📞 +91-9600242268

ebullientcounsellor@gmail.com

You can also follow her on social media

Ebullientcareercounselling

CHAPTER 1

THE REAL MEANING OF SUCCESS

Every one of us loves the word success & we desire to be successful in every aspect of life. There are 4 areas of our life career, family, personal & society where we want to be successful. Out of the four, career is topping the list for most of us, as it gives us financial freedom & helps us to succeed in the rest of the three.

We do everything possible on earth to succeed, starting from joining a course, reading books, attending the webinar, watching informative videos, etc.

Even your purchasing this book today showcases how passionate you are about building a dream career. My friend, you already have the pre-requisite for becoming a

successful person, as successful people say "passion is the foundation to build an empire of success".

Before revealing the secrets, I would like to break a prolonged myth about success.

We believe Success is accomplishing the desired goal, but actually, success is the journey & not the destination. If a person has a worthy predetermined goal & he starts working towards achieving it, he or she is a successful person.

On the other hand, the meaning of failure is "not achieving one's goal & need to improve to achieve", it is as simple as that.

Then, why do we get scared after seeing or hearing the word, 'failure'? It all started from our school days when we first came across the concept of the 'pass' or 'fail' system in our life. It was initially introduced to review students' academic performance, suggest a plan for improvement & help them get back on track with their studies.

But nowadays most of us feel education is the only purpose of our life & take the results close to our heart. We forget that the results which we received were purely based on our performance in that particular subject on that particular date. We need to understand that the result never states "that this person is not qualified forever or can't achieve it throughout his or her life".

Hence, never take any decision purely based on the exam results.

Let me share a success story of a wonderful person, whom I think, you should know………………..

THAT IS YOU

Starting from talking, sitting, walking, reading, writing, cycling, etc...... we all failed initially, but we learned from our mistakes & succeeded. Hence every one of us is already successful.

The 7 Secrets mentioned in the book will transform your life if followed sincerely.

This has helped me to transform my life, and my clients' lives & it will transform yours too.......

CHAPTER 2

SECRET NO.1 SET A DEFINITE GOAL

Definition of Goal

A goal is something we wish to achieve & we need to direct time, resources & efforts to achieve it. The goal might be a thing that we can touch, feel, see or experience. A goal is a vision of the future or desired outcome that an individual envisions, plans, and commits to achieve. By setting deadlines, people attempt to achieve goals in a limited amount of time. Goals fall into different categories, such as education, business, career, health, relationships, personal development & family.

Before getting deep into the concept of goal. Let us understand the difference between Wish, Desire & Goal:-

Wish:- It is a hope for something to happen.

Desire: - It is a strong feeling of wanting to have something.

Goal:- Desire with a plan.

Secret No.1 Set a Definite Goal

In today's world, what most of us have is a wish or a desire & not a goal.

You might feel, that I have a goal Monika, but my dear friends, a goal without an action plan is just a wish……….

People with a goal succeed because they know where they're heading. It's that simple. Whereas on the other hand, unsuccessful people believe that their lives are shaped by circumstances, external forces, things, and events that happen to them by exterior forces.

Consider a ship with the entire journey mapped out and planned. The captain and crew know exactly where the ship is going and how long it will take to get there — it has a specific destination. And it will get there 99% of the time.

Take another ship, similar to the first, but this time with no destination or goal. Let us simply start the engines and let them run. I think you'll agree that if it ever gets out of the harbor, it'll either sink or end up on a deserted beach. It can't go anywhere because it has no direction or destination.

Let us see in detail, why is it Important to set a goal.

Goals Give You Focus

Without a goal, your efforts will be disjointed and frequently confusing. It enables you to zero in on each day's tasks with pinpoint accuracy, eliminating wasted effort and idle movement.

Goals help you measure progress

Tracking your progress towards a goal is only possible if you have set one. Being able to measure progress is hugely rewarding and helps you stay focused, hold your head up high, and keep your energy up. It will also prevent you from going down.

Goals help you stay motivated

It's easy to put off work until tomorrow when there's no goal at stake. For example, consider the life of an athlete. For example, if they need to get in shape for a commonwealth game, they better exercise every day, whether they feel good or not, whether they are in pain or not, whether they be tired or not, and whether they want to do it or not, because they have a purpose. They go to a gym to achieve their goal.

Goals help you overcome procrastination

Procrastination is something everyone including me struggles with from time to time. When you set specific goals in life, what you want to achieve, it helps you to understand, that the act of procrastination is really dangerous.

It has wasted time. It's another day that doesn't get you closer to that goal.

The next time you think about postponing the next step towards your goal, remember an inspirational quote meaning "Only put off until tomorrow what you are ready to die without having done"

Goals get you even more

When you set a goal and achieve it, it gives you a taste of victory. You will want to taste it again. What does that mean? You push yourself to the next rung of the ladder, you challenge yourself to cross another ceiling, and you reach even more.

When you strive for surprising goals, you can accomplish so much more than you ever thought possible.

Goals help you determine what you want in life

Goal setting forces you to think about what you want out of life.

What success do you want to achieve? What is the level of income you want to have? What does your life of convenience look like? What about your dream home?

Once this ultimate goal is determined, break down your desires into mini actionable plans. Hence setting goals can help us live the life we want to live.

Now as we know goal is the key to becoming successful in our life. Let us see how many people set goals & what percentage of them achieve them .

According to recent research, only 20% of people set goals for themselves, which means that the other 80% do not.

What's more unfortunate is that out of the 20% of people who do set goals, only about 30% of them achieve them. That means only one-third of those who set goals achieve them, accounting for 6% of all people.

Another interesting fact

Do you know how many people meet their New Year's resolutions?

Only 8% of people who set New Year's resolutions reach them, which means that 92% fail. 62% give up on their resolutions within a month.

Let us see the "Reasons Why We Fail To Achieve our goals".

Changing focus from rewards to hard work

Before starting the job, we focus on the reward. Then, slowly but surely, we begin to focus more on the hard work (i.e., effort) required to get that reward. The key is to bring our attention back to the reward as often as necessary to succeed.

Goals are undefined

If your goal is to become the next YouTube viral star. Well, that's great, and there's nothing wrong with it, but how do you plan to make it happen? Without a clear definition of your goals, they are just wishy-washy fantasies.

You have set too many goals at a time.

Having multiple goals at once isn't bad. However, if you have so many goals that nothing is ever a priority, you will get poor results everywhere. If you feel like you're never going to complete a task or can't see what has the highest priority, chances are you've set too many goals at once...

Many of us like to think we are multitasking masters. Make sure you don't overload yourself, learn to prioritize and you'll reach your goals faster.

Losing Why Factor

Goals can be set on just about any subject imaginable, but if you don't have a higher goal, it's easy to give up once the initial motivation and enthusiasm wear off. When you understand how important your goal is to you, you can be consistent even when the going gets tough.

It's easy to lose sight of the why factor when working towards a goal, and that can hinder progress. Be sure to regularly review why you have this goal in the first place.

Allowing No-Sayers to doubt the goal.

The bigger the goal, the more people doubt you're achieving it. It's easy to listen to no-Sayers and let their doubts sidetrack and even crash your goals, and that could be why we don't achieve our goals. There will always be critics and haters, and much of that negativity is rooted in jealousy.

Don't let their doubt get the better of you and instead use it as fuel for the fire to establish your focus and move on.

As long as you know the purpose of your goal, ignore the no-Sayers. You can take into account what they say, but make sure you make the final choice.

Fear Of Failure

Failure to achieve a goal due to fear of failure is crippling and can seriously hold you back in life. Nobody wants to fail and a fear of failure is often caused by a desire for perfection.

However, avoiding taking risks is not a healthy way to live. The good news is that by examining why you might be afraid of failing, you can learn to overcome it and avoid allowing it to sabotage your goals.

Example:- Your Author is a first-time author, I also had the fear of failure when I thought of writing a book, I am experienced in counseling, but this is a new domain. But my strong intention to share my knowledge helped me to overcome the fear. Now the result is in front of you. I might not be at my best, but if I don't try how will I perfect this new skill?

A quick update Friends "Happy to share that the book you are reading is #1 Amazon Best Seller in 2 categories & I have become #1 Amazon bestselling author now" This was my goal , before I started this journey of book writing.

Apologies, excuses and more excuses

Apologies are useful when it comes to giving up a goal, but they are also crippling. If you don't keep them in check, apologies can derail whatever goal you're trying to achieve. If you feel like you're about to hit a target, look closely and ask yourself if the reason is valid or just a lame excuse.

Things will go wrong. This is a fact.

If something happens and you don't reach your goal, who do you blame? Your boss making you work late so or maybe the terrible weather that kept you from going to the gym. If it's not your fault, there's nothing you can do, right? Everyone sometimes makes excuses. Finding excuses to explain "why a goal isn't worth pursuing or why we failed" is often easier than continuing towards the goal. While some excuses may very well be valid, others are just a total subterfuge.

We can overcome these challenges & achieve our goal by applying an effective goal-setting method. Here I am sharing the one which has helped me personally.

10 Steps to Effective Goal Setting:
Believe in the process

The first step in goal setting is to have absolute belief in the process. If you are not confident in yourself and your abilities, you might as well forget about your attempt to achieve your goals. If in doubt, look around. Everything you see around once started as a goal in someone's mind.

Write it down

To achieve the objective, you need to plan your attack. Write down your goals and the planned dates for their implementation and evaluation. This can be the key to success because writing down your goals will position you as a creator. If you neglect this step, you may continue to forget about them or you may not find it important. Having them somewhere you see them every day will help you reaffirm their importance and increase your chances of reaching them.

Set specific goals

A goal is much more likely to be achieved when it comes to specific facts and events. If your directions are vague, they can be misinterpreted and easily skipped. Specific goals give speed and precision to your training program.

Set measurable goals

If your goals can meet concrete criteria, you can measure progress towards achieving them. If you identify what you will see, hear and feel when you have achieved your goal, you can feel that you have achieved something tangible. To set effective goals, you need to break your goal down into measurable elements.

Set achievable goals

While there's nothing wrong with shooting for the stars, it's important to consider whether the goal applies to you and your lifestyle. If you don't have the time, money, or experience to achieve something, you will fail and you will certainly be unhappy. For the most effective goal setting, be sure to carefully plan your milestones and set a realistic timeline that will allow you to complete those milestones.

Set realistic goals

Nothing demotivates more than not being able to achieve something you set out to do. To be realistic, your goal should represent a goal you want and can work towards. You are the only one who can determine how substantial your goal should be, but you need to make sure there is a real chance that you can achieve it under the right circumstances.

Set goals with a timeline

Any set goals must be grounded within a time frame. If you don't have a deadline, there will be no sense of urgency.

Make a preliminary plan of everything you are going to do and when you want to do it. Introducing deadlines helps you and your team work towards it and creates motivation that can keep morale up. However, creating deadlines can be a tricky and sensitive task. On the one hand, being too strict about the timelines aspect of goal setting can be motivating, but it can also have the opposite effect and be demotivating if you don't check the timeline boxes.

Stay accountable

When you're working towards a goal, it inevitably becomes difficult. When you face adversity, you have to hold yourself accountable. Talking to your family and friends about your goals can help you take on the responsibility you need and muster the support system to give you a boost. By staying accountable in your day-to-day life, you'll also surround yourself with constant encouragement from those who track your progress.

Don't be afraid to get peer support

When entering a new organization, learning from those around you is crucial. You should ask for support from a peer, senior, or manager, or have a mentor, it will help you hone your skills & will bring you one step closer to your goal.

Continually assess your progress

Over time, our goals are constantly changing and evolving. The result may not look like what we originally intended; However, sometimes that can be a good thing. Learn from your mistakes, constantly assess your progress along your goal-setting journey.

Merely thinking about a goal increases the success rate to 43%. Are you curious to know, what are the other ways to increase the success rate of a goal?

Here are a few simple techniques, which helped me to become a career coach:-

Writing down your goal

By writing your goals, we take them out of our minds and make them visible. In turn, it creates a vision in our minds of how we want to be in the future.

Writing down our goals, helps us to focus our attention and provides short-term motivation and excitement.

This clarity allows us to filter out things, activities, and people that don't support our goals, this leads to increased productivity.

Success rate increases to 61%.

Sharing Your Goal

Sharing your goals with the right people (your trainer, mentor or manager) and publicly sharing your progress (like social media), helps you to keep yourself accountable. It also makes you more motivated.

Success rate increases to 64%

Visualizing your goal. Visualize your goal twice a day for a total of 10 minutes. It's most effective in the moments you wake up and the moments just before you go to sleep. This will help you engage the subconscious mind to focus on your desired outcome. It could be achieved by creating a vision board or mind movie to make it impactful.

Success rate Increases to 73%.

Examples Of Definite Goals

\# I will study Math daily for 1 hour in the afternoon Monday to Friday for 5 weeks.

\# I plan to finish a 50,000-word novel in 5 months, on Jan 30th. This will be accomplished by writing 2,500 words per week.

\# I will obtain the confidence to give a public speech by practicing daily in front of the mirror for 10 minutes & participating in the public speaking forum every Sunday for 5 minutes for the next 4 months.

\# I will begin a Facebook Ads course tomorrow and start investing 25% of my business profits into paid campaigns within 2 weeks. I will continue to learn and invest in Facebook Ads to double my sales within 2 months.

Famous Example of achieving a goal

Legend Actor Rajnikanth:- He is the superstar of the Tamil Cinema Industry. Popularly known as Thalaiva among fans. He was born as Shivaji Rao Gaekwad to a Marathi family in Karnataka, India. He was a bus conductor, His desire to be an actor pushed him to take up acting and enter the Indian film industry.

Captain Cool MS Dhoni:- Mahendra Singh Dhoni, one of India's greatest cricketers, has not had much interest in cricket since childhood.

Dhoni first played badminton and football at the district and club levels. While playing football as a goalkeeper, he was chosen by his coach to play as a wicketkeeper at the local cricket club. As he began to hold wickets regularly for the local club, he honed his cricketing skills and was regularly capped in club cricket. Dhoni comes from a lower middle-class family and his father Pan Singh was employed at MECON at the junior level. To support himself and his family, Dhoni accepted the job of a rail ticket examiner or TTE at Indian Railways. Dhoni worked as a train ticket examiner from 2000 to 2003 and was selected for the Indian cricket team in 2004. Rest is history.

CHAPTER 3

SECRET NO. 2 BREAKING OUT OF CONFORMITY

Let us understand **what is conformity**.

This is the act of matching behaviors, attitudes, and beliefs to other people, group norms, or political ideologies. People in society prefer to conform to existing rules, practices, and beliefs rather than create new ones. Although this occurs in large or small groups, it frequently results in social pressure or unconscious influences.

Conformity arises from the need for security from a group of people of a similar age, educational level, religion and culture, and is also known as groupthink. This frequently disregards the realistic assessment of other societal and personal beliefs. Failure to comply with these societal pressure risks rejection. While it is generally associated with youth culture, it affects people of all ages.

When do we conform?

It is something that occurs regularly in our social environments. We are sometimes aware of our behavior, but most of the time it happens without much thought or awareness on our part. In some cases, we agree with things we disagree with or act in ways we know we shouldn't. The best example is people going along with the group, even when they know the group is wrong.

Why do people conform?

Things are easier when you conform.

In general, people tend to act sanely most of the time when everyone else is acting similarly. You're confident that you're probably right because something that everyone does has been tried and tested by, well, everyone. Since everyone is doing it, all current systems are designed to support it, making it a streamlined procedure that everyone can assist you with and relate to. And even if you are mistaken, everyone else is, so it doesn't make you stand out adversely. On the other hand, if you're the only one doing something, you have nothing other than your intuition to right. Not only will no one else have done it before, but many people will think you're crazy for not conforming and will try to convince you of that before you go any further, which means you won't be able to get those people to objectively consider whether you're right or not and will have to figure it out for yourself.

You often have to jump through many additional hurdles that you would have unnecessarily adapted to, as each system has already solved the human-friendliness issues on the path to confirmation. And if you get it wrong, which is already much more likely when you're the only one doing it, you end up looking ridiculous and being scolded by all the people who were too scared to break the pattern and will taunt "I told you so".

That's why people conform.

Potential Pitfall of Conformity

While it is often advantageous to fit in with a group, conformity can also have negative consequences. If you have to change your appearance or personality to fit in a gang, it will lower your self-esteem.

Allowing peer pressure to influence you may lead to risky or illegal behavior, such as underage drinking. Conformity may also result in a bystander effect, in which joining the group means failing to intervene when someone is in need.

A desire to fit in may also limit your ability to be open to new ideas or arguments. Conforming to a group can even lead to prejudiced feelings or actions.

A short real-time story explaining conformity in career:- Recently I received a call from a final year EEE graduate, stating that I am not liking this B.Tech course. I asked him what made him to choose engineering, he said my dad asked me to join (who was an engineer). During the conversation I asked him how many siblings do you have, he said 1 younger brother & we just got him enrolled in EEE, I asked him whether it was his brother's choice, and he said no, we chose on his behalf, as engineering is the best career with the highest package..........

People are acting like everyone else, without knowing where & why they are going.

I hope now you understand what is conformity & when & how we are supposed to take charge of our careers.

Famous People Examples:-

Captain Gopinath, the founder of Air Deccan, which revolutionized Indian air travel, comes from a humble family. Captain Gopinath was the second of eight children born to a school teacher. After completing his education, Gopinath was commissioned into the Indian Army for an eight-year term. He became a farmer after retiring from the military, establishing a sustainable farm, opening an Enfield dealership, and running an Udipi hotel. Captain Gopinath finally started Deccan Aviation, a helicopter charter service - which later became the launch pad for Air Deccan - after many ventures, failures, and adversities.

CHAPTER 4

SECRET NO.3 BECOME PERSEVERANT

What Does Perseverance Mean?

In its simplest form, perseverance is the act of working towards your goal despite challenges and setbacks. It is the perseverance you show even when you are late in achieving goals or accomplishments. People with long-term goals often lose focus & it's hard not to lose motivation and enthusiasm after a certain point; However, perseverance teaches you to keep working hard until you succeed.

No matter what challenges come your way or how long it takes for you to complete the task, stay relentless and pursue the goal you have set for yourself. It's an important quality in life because it keeps you in the game when everything else says it's time to end it. Perseverance will help you achieve your dreams, goals, and visions in life.

Why Is Perseverance Important?

People who show perseverance are more likely to be successful in life, especially in professional life. Perseverance is a sign of getting out of your comfort zone and staying focused on your efforts. It also means that you have a growth mindset, that is the belief that, through your efforts you can develop essential qualities. This is a very valuable quality that organizations actively look for when hiring people.

Why do we need to develop this quality:-
It leads to mastery

You may not know how to do something, even if you are passionate about it. It is perseverance that will help you try to pursue something, as well as do your best.

Rome was not built in a day; you have to be patient because hard work will pay off in the end. Prolonged effort over time can even lead you to master a new skill. You can excel as long as you remain determined.

You become resilient

Suppose you were turned down after seven job interviews. You can stop looking for a job or refuse to give up. Persevering people don't give up easily. They will continue to face challenges and work hard. That's why you become resilient as you go through hardships and keep stepping out of your comfort zone. You also continue to grow emotionally.

Teaches how to cope with the crisis

Perseverance teaches you to focus on solutions rather than problems. For example, if something goes wrong, persistent individuals will find ways to mitigate a crisis. They know how to stay calm and carry on. In other words, they look at the bigger picture and don't leave a situation or responsibility unfinished. The importance of perseverance is that it makes you optimistic about the future. You learn not to give up because you believe the power stays in your hands as long as you hold on to it.

How to develop perseverance?

Refuse the Call to Quit:-

The first step in building perseverance is to reject the urge to give up or quit. If you can't do something, give yourself some time. Start over the next day. Remind yourself why you are doing it and the ultimate goal you want to achieve.

Make a Plan of Action:-

A detailed action plan can help you stay focused on each goal. You must be accountable for your journey from start to completion. The main benefit of the plan is that it makes you accountable and helps you keep track of your progress. The more you check, the easier it is to stay motivated.

Get Obsessed with Self-development:-

The core of perseverance is getting out of your comfort zone. You have to make peace with the fact that you have to work on self-improvement. Setting higher standards of excellence for yourself is a good start. If you continue to build perseverance, you will continue to grow as a well-rounded person. Perseverance is a skill that employers value because they need people who can overcome difficult circumstances.

Famous Examples of Perseverance
Dr. APJ. Abdul Kalam:-

Dr. APJ Abdul Kalam, an Indian scientist and the eleventh president of India from 2002 to 2007, faced insurmountable difficulties on his way to becoming the leader of a nation. Dr. Abdul Kalam was born into a Tamil Muslim family; his father Jainulabdeen was a boat owner and his mother Ashiamma was a housewife. Dr. Abdul Kalam comes from a poor family and started working at a young age to supplement the family income by distributing newspapers after school to contribute financially to his father's income. In his school years, he had average grades, but he was a hardworking student with an interest in mathematics. Even during his senior project while in college, the principal was dissatisfied with the lack of progress and threatened to withdraw his scholarship unless the project was completed within the next three days. He then worked tirelessly on his project and met the deadline, which impressed the Principal. From that moment on, Dr.Kalam joined the Aeronautical Development Establishment of Defense Research and Development Organization (DRDO) as a scientist and led the organization. The rest we all know.

CHAPTER 5

SECRET NO.4 EMBRACE FAILURE

Failure is the first step or step to success, even in the dictionary failure comes first, then success.

F.A.I.L stands for First Attempt to Learn.

The number of times you fail towards your goal, the success rate increases. No one has seen success without failure otherwise there is no joy in life for the success you feel after struggling a lot to achieve your dream.

What exactly is embracing failure?

Finkelstein sums it up quite simply: "It's the point of positively embracing failure...it allows you to overcome negatives and disappointments and shift your mindset from 'failure is bad' to 'Failure can be good ' and here it is 'changing the way to make it a tool in itself'.

Why is it important to accept failure?

Failure is something we should embrace rather than avoid. By failing at something, we have the opportunity to identify weak points that need to be corrected to face future challenges. Failure is the process of becoming stronger as a person.

How should we embrace our failure?

Failure is an inevitable part of our life. Sometimes we learn from our mistakes and sometimes we just don't know what went wrong. By accepting failure, you accept yourself and your circumstances as part of life. It's an opportunity for growth, but it's not a measure of your future or your self-worth. Although some things are beyond your control, failure and success often go hand in hand - success is usually the result of past failures. Accepting failure can lead to success down the road.

Let us see healthy ways to deal with failure
1. Embrace your emotions

Failure involves a variety of emotions: shyness, fear, anger, sadness, and shame, just to name a few. These feelings are uncomfortable and many people will go to great lengths to escape emotional distress.

So go ahead and embrace your emotions. Recognize how you feel and let yourself feel a little bad. Label your emotions while allowing yourself to experience them. For example, you might think "I'm disappointed" or "I'm sorry it didn't work out."

Recognize unhealthy attempts to reduce pain

You might be tempted to say, "I didn't want that job anyway," but minimizing your pain won't make it go away. Distracting yourself or filling the void you feel with food, drugs or alcohol will also not cure your pain. These things will only give you temporary relief.

Recognize the unhealthy ways you try to avoid or minimize the pain in your life. If you turn to coping mechanisms that do more harm than good, your situation will only get worse.

Practice a healthy coping skill

Calling a friend, taking a bubble bath, going for a walk, practicing deep breathing, or playing with your pet are just a few examples of healthy ways to manage your pain. However, not all coping skills work for everyone, so it's important to figure out what works for you.

" Your author simply listens to music for half an hour, feels relaxed & gets back to work with a positive mindset".

Recognize irrational beliefs about failure

You might have developed irrational beliefs about failure at some point in your life. Maybe you think failure means you're bad or that you'll never succeed. Or maybe you think no one will love you if you fail. These types of beliefs are inaccurate and can prevent you from doing things that you can be successful at. Identify your irrational beliefs that may be influencing your feelings and behavior & keep a check on it..

Develop realistic thoughts about failure

Failure is a signal that I am challenging myself to do something new & difficult.

I can handle failures.

I can learn from my mistakes.

You may need to repeat a positive statement or affirmation like – "I am good at learning new skills", to wipe off negative thoughts or strengthen yourself so that you can bounce back.

Accept a reasonable level of responsibility

It is important to take a specific level of responsibility for your failure. If you take too much, you may blame yourself unnecessarily. On the other hand, blaming other people or unfortunate circumstances for your failures will prevent your learning .

When you think about your failures, look for explanations, not excuses. Identify the reasons for your failure and recognize what you can do differently next time.

Research Famous Failures

From Thomas Edison to Walt Disney, famous failure stories. Spend time researching famous people who have failed. You'll probably find they've done it so many times along the way. Most successful people continue to fail regularly. Actors are rejected for roles, athletes are removed from the team and entrepreneurs are rejected for deals.

Study what they did to recover.

You may be learning skills that can help you in your life. It can be helpful to see that failure is something everyone has to contend with.

Ask yourself what you can learn.

Failure can be an amazing teacher if you are open to learning. Did you make a mistake, did you make a whole bunch of mistakes?

Think about how you can do it differently next time. So, you make sure your failure has become a life lesson that helped you learn something. Instead of seeing failure as a burden on you, see it as a stepping stone to your goals. Make a plan to move forward. Once you identify your mistakes and what you can learn from them, you are ready to make a plan to move forward.

Remember, dwelling on your problems or repeating your mistakes will block you. Stop thinking that "I am a failure" and start thinking "I can win". With your new lessons, think about what you will do differently next time. Make a plan that will help you apply the information you gain.

Face your fear of failure

If you've spent most of your life avoiding being jobless, it can be downright scary when it finally happens. However, facing your fears can be the key to reducing discomfort. Train yourself to come out of your comfort area. Do things you might get rejected for or try new things you might fail at. Over time, you'll learn that failure isn't as bad as you might think. It will help you deal with your fear of failure in a way that can be productive and help you achieve your goals.

Famous People Example

Actor Amitabh Bachchan Aka BIG B:

He said in an interview

"In the year 2000, as the whole world celebrated the new century, I celebrated my disastrous fate. There were no movies, no money, no business, a million lawsuits against and the taxman had ordered the seizure of my house." - This quote from Amitabh Bachchan at the turn of the century gives insight into the adversity faced by

Amitabh Bachchan when he was in his late 50s. He now remembers how he felt like there was a sword hanging from his head the whole time and how many nights he was sleepless. Around this time, Amitabh got up early one morning and went to see Yash Chopra. He told him he was bankrupt, had no movies, and his house had been seized by creditors. Yash Chopra offered AB an amazing role in his film Mohabattein. Amitabh also started doing commercials and television programs. At that time, he had a big breakthrough, thanks to Kaun Banega Crorepati; it propelled him to national fame and helped reverse his fate.

CHAPTER 6

SECRET NO.5 STOP WORRYING

Are you worried about something right now? You are likely to be worried about several things. Some people are certainly more worried than others, but we all tend to worry at least a little.

According to the research, " About 40% of what we worry about never happens! 30% is in the past and cannot be helped. However, 12% is none of our business and 10% is about illness, real or imagined. Only 8% worth worrying about. "

Mackay puts things in perspective! 92% of what we normally worry about never happens, can't be helped, or shouldn't worry us. Can you imagine being 92% less worried than you are now? How carefree and refreshing life looks!

If only it were that easy ... worrying is an emotion, and as much as we would like it to be, emotions can't be turned on and off like a switch. Our emotions can be easily influenced - by people, circumstances, music, movies, food, medicine, etc.

But there is no "ON or OFF switch". So how do we stop worrying? Wisdom and perspective are essential! 40% of what worries us never happens. When you start worrying about a negative possibility, remember that it's very likely that it will never happen, so why waste time worrying? 30% of our worries have already passed. Stop worrying about it. You can't change it - accept the facts and let it be. 12% of what we worry about is none of our business. Why bother about something that is not significant to us in any way. Remind yourself it's none of your business and forget it! 10% of our worries are related to illness. While illness can be a very real concern & worrying does not improve it. Take the necessary steps to prevent or treat the disease, but don't worry unnecessarily. And the last 8%? Well, worry if you have to, but remember that worrying - whatever it is - is useless if you don't act.

Here's a pretty good thumb rule: if you can do something about it, then it's worth worrying about - but don't just worry about it - do something, take action & make a difference.

Why do we worry?

While many of us are intuitively aware that worry makes us feel anxious and upset, research shows that we still tend to worry about issues in our lives. One major reason is that we may worry about feeling emotionally prepared for negative outcomes.

How we can stop worrying:-
Plan Some Worry Time:-

Paying attention to your worries may seem counterintuitive, but research has shown that scheduling time to worry can help reduce anxious thoughts and improve sleep.

First, set yourself a time of day when you can take 20 minutes to do nothing but worry. Some people prefer to worry in the morning to relieve themselves early in the day. Others prefer to postpone their worries until the evening to free themselves from all the worries that have accumulated during the day.

Whatever time of day you choose, it's important to spend time focusing on your worrying thoughts. Worry will always occur at times outside of your scheduled worry time. If they do, acknowledge them briefly, but only give them your full attention during the scheduled rush hour.

By engaging in rumination sessions, you may begin to find that you are in control of your worries. By scheduling your worry time, you can break the chain of frequent worry you experience throughout the day.

Also, by focusing on your concerns for only a certain amount of time, you may find that they are not as urgent as you once thought. This can free your mind to focus on more productive thoughts.

Overcome Procrastination:-

Putting time and energy into your worries instead of taking action to solve your problems can become a form of procrastination. Many people spend time mulling over what to do instead of completing their homework. Also, putting off the responsibilities you are dealing with will only add to your worries.

Avoid procrastinating by making a list of all the things you need to do. By writing down a to-do list, you can get all those anxious thoughts out of your head and put them on paper. Whenever you are worried about something else you need to have a glance of your to-do- list, it can get you back on the path to productivity. Instead of worrying about what needs to be done, focus on completing each task you've written down on your list.

Talk it Out:-

You may find relieved if you share your thoughts and concerns with a trusted friend or family member. Loved ones can be a great source of support as they provide you with empathy and understanding. Friends and family can also give you valuable advice and give you a different perspective on your problems.

Sometimes it can be difficult for even the most patient loved ones to always be available to listen to your concerns. If you are chronically worried, you should consider getting help from a professional who treats anxiety disorders. Additional resources and social support can be found at your place of worship, group therapy, online support forums or local anxiety support groups.

Journaling thoughts:-

Many people are struggling with feelings of loneliness and isolation. Maybe you feel like you have no one to discuss your issues and concerns with. However, a journal may be all you need to process your thoughts, feelings, emotions, and worries.

Journaling is a powerful and effective way to connect with your inner self. By writing in a journal, you can process your difficult emotions, find solutions to your problems, and change your perceptions and concerns. Getting started with journaling can be as simple as spending time each day writing down your inner thoughts. You can focus on addressing all of your concerns, writing them down as they arise and giving yourself the freedom to fully express how you feel.

Turn your thoughts around:-

Worry is a negative thought pattern that can contribute to anxiety symptoms. Negative thinking is usually a learned habit that can affect your mood and anxiety.

Since negative thinking tends to develop over time, it can be unlearned and replaced with more positive attitudes.

Reversing your worries and other negative thoughts involves acknowledgment, reality check and substitution. First, start by recognizing how often you worry during the day. It may also be helpful to jot down these thoughts on a piece of paper as they emerge. Next, examine your worries and ask yourself if you are being realistic. Try to look at the other side of the worry or the negative thought. For example, if you fear others won't accept you because of your fear, ask yourself if that's true. Do people only accept those who are completely fearless? Do you want to be friends with someone who can't accept you for who you are?

Finally, replace these negative thoughts and worries with more realistic statements. For example, you start thinking, that it's ok even if not everyone accepts that you are an anxious person, but you work towards your health & fitness & most importantly accept the way you are.

Practice Relaxation techniques:-

It is difficult to feel anxious in a state of relaxation. Learning to relax can be made easier by using relaxation techniques. These activities are designed to help you release tension throughout your body and get rid of worrying thoughts. Next time worry is on your mind, try one of these relaxation techniques, it has helped me & my clients to get back to the positive mindset:

* Deep breathing

* Meditation

* Visualization &

* Yoga

CHAPTER 7

SECRET NO.6 BEAT YOUR SMARTPHONE ADDICTION

Let us see a few recent world trends, which fueled our addiction to mobile. But the data shared below will help us to reflect & take the required action to get the situation in control.

When the pandemic hit the globe in 2020 mobile usage increased and continued to increase in 2021 & 2022.

According to a recent report, Indians spent more than 699 billion hours on mobile devices, out of the total of 3.8 trillion hours spent on mobile devices around the world. With so much consumption, India ranks second after China and ahead of the United States.

The numbers are not surprising as India is the second largest smartphone market in the world, contributing to that cheap and convenient mobile internet. But it highlights the growing use and dependence on mobile devices as the primary electronic device for entertainment, communications, education, games, finance, and more. It is not over yet…

Would you like to know a few shocking facts about mobile usage by Annie App research:-

\# India ranks second in app downloads. In 2021, there were 26.7 billion downloads on the Google Play Store and App Store.

\# Financial apps had over 1 billion downloads in India last year. Job search apps Apna for India with 17.7 million downloads.

\# The most downloaded app in India in 2021 was Instagram.

\# The app with the highest consumer spending was Hot star.

\# WhatsApp had the highest number of monthly active users.

\# A total of 2 million new apps and games for iOS and Android devices were launched in 2021.

\# The average time spent on social media per day by a global internet user is 2 hours and 27 minutes.

Emerging markets continue to spend most of their time on social networks on a regular day. This may be because these markets tend to have a younger population, with the 16-24 age segment driving growth across the globe. Nigeria has spent most of its time on social networks, spending more than four hours a day in the digital social sphere. Filipinos typically spent nearly the same amount of time per day on social media sites, while Indians and Chinese logged around 2.5 hours & 2 hours per day, respectively.

Countries with aging populations have shown shorter use of social media. On a typical day in Japan, people only spend 45 minutes staying in touch on social networks. Germany only posts slightly higher numbers, with users spending an hour and twenty minutes on social media every day, while the UK and the US both spend nearly two hours a day on social media.

Few more mind-boggling facts

\# According to research done in Washington, we tap, swipe, and click our smartphones an average of 2617 times a day.

\# For heavier users, 5,427 touches per day.

\# The average user ran 76 separate phone sessions per day.

\# Heavy users averaged 132 sessions per day.

\# Long usage sessions are rare, but mainly Netflix and reading.

\# People prefer lots of small sessions with breaks in between.

\# The keys explode at 7 a.m. and increase almost continuously until dinner. According to the study, 87 percent of participants checked their phones at least once between midnight and 5 am.

\# Social media posts and apps accounted for 26% and 22% of interactions.

\# Facebook had the most taps at 15 percent. Half of all telephone responses occur within 3 minutes of the previous one.

And the effects of this use are overwhelming:

\# Decrease in call quality.

\# Problems with short-term memory and problem-solving.

\# Negative effects on our sleeping habits.

\# This leads to more negativity, stress and less emotional recovery in young children.

\# The increase in obesity and depression is alarming due to smartphone addiction.

Secret No.6 Beat Your Smartphone Addiction

You would think that, given the stats and what we know about cell phone usage, it would be easy to put it down and walk away. But I can confirm that the fight against addiction to technology is real.

As a parent of two children making a living online in this modern world, I am very familiar with the addictive nature of mobile devices and how great the internal struggle is to reap the rewards of our smartphones without falling prey to the intentionally compelling design.

Nor do I miss the ironic fact that many of you are reading this book on your mobile phones.

Mobiles are good and useful … that's why you can read this book now. But we know all too well that they also have the potential to become a negative presence in our lives if we let them.

So how can we keep cell phone usage consistent with our lives? What are some tools or ideas to help us reduce cell phone usage?

The scariest thing about smartphone addiction is that it can affect our physical and mental health, our relationships and productivity. These smartphones are like drug or gambling addictions and offer an escape from reality.

Human beings are naturally sensitive to distractions. With smartphones, we have a world of distractions at our fingertips. It's time to recognize that our devices can negatively impact our lives and we need to do something about it.

In the past, cell phones were just a means of communication. Now it's GPS, cameras, game consoles, health trackers and the list goes on. We use our devices for everything from waiting in line at the grocery store, reading the news, filing our taxes, or controlling the thermostat. We don't just use our smartphones for everything, we rely on them.

The effects of smartphone addiction don't end there; Our overuse of technology has completely changed the way we communicate and interact with others. Instead of having real face-to-face conversations with the people in our lives, we often hide behind a screen. While technology can be a useful tool to keep us connected, we need to be careful when and how we use it.

4 Proven ways to break smartphone addiction

Schedule 1 day per week

This is by far the most common approach I see among people today who have taken deliberate steps to restrict cell phone use. Pick one day a week (usually a Saturday and Sunday) and put your phone aside. That's it, get used to it.

Use apps to increase self-control

There are apps for almost every problem in life. There are even wonderful apps that have been developed to help us limit our time on our devices. Here are some of my favorites:

Moment:- Moment helps you to use your phone healthily through short daily exercises.

Flipd:- Block distracting apps for maximum focus.

Screen time:- Set daily usage limits for your phone or specific apps.

Charge your phone away from your bed

Want to know the best way to stop your kids from using their phones? Do not allow them to charge their phone in their room. Want to know how to stay off your phone? Do not charge it in your bedroom.

Many of the negative effects of overuse (poor sleep & impaired communication) can be eliminated by keeping your cell phone out of your bedroom. As with many of the items on this list, this is a principle that I have personally found useful.

Are you constantly texting, surfing the web, emailing, using apps, and playing games? Depending on how much time and effort you put into these situations, you may have a cell phone overuse problem. Excessive use of your cell phone can lead to reduced quality of personal relationships and a lack of productivity in daily life.

Change your phone settings.

Some settings on your phone may notify you whenever you receive an email or Facebook notification. Be sure to turn them off! This will reduce how often your phone will turn off or vibrate. This way you won't be notified every time something happens.

What triggers the usage of a cell phone?
Fulfilling social tasks differently.

Much of our desire to be on the phone comes from our innate and evolutionary urge to be social beings. However, there are other options for being social that can be more beneficial and satisfying in the long run.

Instead of texting, you can write a letter or meet up with a friend for coffee or a meal.

Instead of taking your photos on Instagram, invite a family member and show them your memories. This type of connection can increase the quality of intimacy.

Replace your habits.

Think about all the reasons you use your phone (gaming, texting, phone calls). Some of these habits may be necessary for your work and daily life (perhaps work email, etc.), while others could disrupt your life if they distract you from your normal interactions and responsibilities. Try to replace each of these disruptive habits with more productive, social and quality experiences.

If one of your problems is playing excessive games on your phone, consider an alternative, e.g. By inviting a friend to a board game. If you spend too much time looking at social media profiles, meet a close friend or family member and ask them what's going on in their life (instead of just reading about it online).

How to limit cell phone usage

Social support is a crucial part of mental health. Having a positive social network creates feelings of security and belonging. These components are important when considering limiting cell phone usage, as usage is likely to be based at least in part on the social connection (such as text messaging, and use of social apps). Just tell your family and friends that you think you are using your cell phone excessively and that you are working to cut back. You can indicate that you will appreciate their assistance in this process. You can also ask them to give specific suggestions and include them in your plan. For example, ask them to only call or text you at certain times of the day. Ask for advice. Your family members know you personally and can help you come up with a concrete plan to reduce your phone use.

CHAPTER 8

SECRET NO.7 THE POWER OF ASKING FOR HELP

There are times in our lives when we feel completely helpless and powerless.

Nobody likes to be in a state of need, but as silly as it sounds, we often feel too embarrassed, too shy or too proud to ask for help.

You may have grown accustomed to it after someone teased you when you were a child. But the truth is that many people would rather stay in a situation that is not good for them and feel unhappy than seeking help.

But it sounds strange to say that asking for help is a skill, right?

But just like any other skill, you get better at it as you practice asking for help. With a little patience, you will become better at overcoming your shyness and pride and at accepting help from others. By getting used to asking for and receiving help from others, you can not only improve your current situation but also benefit in other ways.

Let's see why it's so powerful and important to mastering it and the useful products you get by practicing it.

Asking for help is a strength, not a weakness admitting that you are struggling and that you need someone's help to move forward is something that only willing people who are committed to their goals. Only confident people can admit they need help & only strong people can reveal their vulnerability to improve their situation, and even the toughest man in the world speaks openly about the fact that there is great power in vulnerability. I know that's easier said than done. Trying to recover from a bad breakup, letting go of a painful setback, losing a loved one or feeling stuck in life can be extremely difficult.

But you must recognize that by sharing your vulnerability and exposing the parts you are not proud of to others, you become stronger. You accept yourself enough to show the world that you are not perfect. You show the real you, not a character.

And what is the alternative? Continue to suffer? Getting stuck in the same place without moving forward? You only live once and every minute you waste being guilty of

Secret No. 7 The Power of Asking For Help

your problems and not being able to move on is a minute that prevents you from improving your situation and living a better life. External support can only make you stronger, so what do you have to lose?

Explaining your problem to someone else is very effective. Getting rid of a problem by sharing it with someone can be a huge relief. Talking out loud about your problems can often greatly reduce them, and explaining your problem to someone else can help clarify the issue. The dark, unsettling, ambiguous mass of a problem in your mind and heart always seems worse than it is. However, when you share a problem, you naturally try to articulate it so that the other person understands what you are going through and this processing and articulation can provide a logical framework for your situation. Now, that's not some big, vague cloud of negativity: it's something tangible that you can take one step at a time. You have to play a different song and hear a different perspective. Each one of us have specific skills and abilities, and someone else's big picture can make you see everything through a completely different prism, giving you new insights and solutions you might not otherwise have.

You don't have to carry the weight of the world on your shoulders, you don't have to carry it all alone. Being alone is difficult and sometimes you feel overwhelmed by everything that has to happen to you, but you know that

1 + 1 = 2, so why not? By consulting with someone else, you will greatly increase your chances. Don't you want to increase your chances?

When you expose your vulnerability, you are authentic, something that is rare in our daily life. Seeing and feeling something real and natural, this authenticity will deepen your intimacy with the people around you. When you share a little part of yourself that no one has ever seen, people will feel closer to you than before. And those closer, deeper relationships are a tremendous power multiplier, a solid foundation for meeting future challenges and your support team for life.

Great side effects

By being vulnerable & authentic, you connect with your true self, with your purpose, with your "why". This connection is the secret of perseverance and will help you overcome any obstacles that come your way. If your "why" is strong enough, you can overcome any "how".

Being authentic allows you to recognize people who are not, and this gives you a great advantage in your personal, business and work life.

As we are nearing the end of the book… You all might have a question now,

"**Everything sounds great Monika**, but how am I going to apply the learning in my current situation & build a successful career, as I do realize that I need support to achieve my goal, what should I do next".

My friend, it is not just only getting support, it is getting the support from the right person, which eventually reduces the time, energy consumed & no. of failures encountered by you & in-turn will help you achieve your career goal faster. And when I say the right person, he or she has to be reliable, available, knowledgeable, qualified & experienced to support you. And I can confidently conclude through my experience, that a Career Coach is an ideal person. Experienced Career Coaches can support any person irrespective of their age & stage of their career in the best way.

Anyone who desires to progress in their career can connect for a free discovery call with me, your career coach Monika will be more than happy to guide you towards your dream career.

See you all with my upcoming book, which will be about the journey of a small-town housewife becoming a global coach"

CLIENT TESTIMONIALS

Millions of people are working hard but only a few are working hard in the right direction. It is important to set a path before we start our journey in life and Ebullient career counseling has helped in finding the right direction to channel my efforts into. It has been an intelligible experience going through my career counseling with my mentor, Monika ma'am. Her vibrant and friendly energy was the life and soul of the sessions I had with her and I loved every second of it. It was not just trying to make a list of careers that would suit me the best but also understanding who I am and what I truly want. She made me realize how important recognizing one's aim in life was at an early stage to avoid regrets in the future. She made me see how knowing myself is the first step to picking a career. The sessions were highly motivating and encouraging. We kept working at it until I was sure of what I wanted to take up as a career. She was always so very patient with me and we built a great bond together. No words could summarize my gratitude towards Monika ma'am and the tremendous help she had been in helping me pick a career. Deciding to take up career counseling had been no doubt one of the best decisions of my life and I was blessed with an amazing mentor. I have gained so much from our sessions. I shall always remember her words of advice that will guide me through life. I know I just sent you the review but I just wanted to say it again, Thank you, ma'am. You can't imagine how much our sessions have helped me. I have really bad anxiety issues and I would overthink all the time about what am i gonna do in my life and that I don't just wanna do anything I wanna be happy in what I do and make money. Researching on Google was like being flooded without knowing to swim. If anything, it made me even more anxious and I'd get sick so frequently because when I'm overthinking I don't eat very well and that is never good. My head would feel so overwhelmed with worries about school future career scholarships going abroad University admissions all at the same time, it was suffocating. Talking to you and working with you and finally figuring out what I wanted in life…it was like a release. Like the weight of the world was off my shoulders. I couldn't stop my tears; I was beyond happy. I have finally stopped running in every direction and focusing on one thing at a time. I'll make this work ma'am. Thanks to you. You're an amazing human being and you're doing a wonderful job helping people find purpose in their lives. Thanks a million ☒

-Srishti – Durgapur (West Bengal)

Ebullient career counselling - Before attending these counselling classes I was doubtful about choosing my career after the 12th. I have taken PCM for 11th and 12th and was getting confused among various fields. The counselling sessions helped me to know myself even better. The personality test was of great help to guide me in choosing the best career path for me because before choosing a career it is very important to first know yourself, know what you like and dislike and then proceed. My career counsellor, Monika was the one who helped me to overcome this confusion. The sessions with her were wonderful. It never felt like I was talking to an advisor but it felt as if I'm talking to a friend. I give my heartfelt gratitude to her for always adjusting with me to finalize the timings for the session. She was always ready to help me out at any point in time to clear all the doubts be it early morning or late at night. The detailed description for each career field favorable for me from top to bottom was really helpful. I would recommend to every student who is going through the same state as I was to join the Ebullient Counselling session. It will surely prove beneficial for you and clear all your doubts. Thank you Monika Ma'am it was a pleasure to interact with you 😊 ♡.

– **Anushka Dutta (Kolkata)**

The session we had was very informative. I was someone who was struggling from finding my dream job and I was quite giving up on the career opportunities available. But you found out what the problem was, and that was quite a revelation for me. Thanks for putting back the motivation Monika! I enjoyed the session, moreover, you made me feel very comfortable and relaxed, like friends! I'm looking forward to the career growth I'll encounter and ill surely want you to be my Guide. Thank you again!

– Gokul Ram (Kerala/Sweden)

Thank you so much Monika ma'am ♡ An excellent counselor, She provides both a great mix of listening, speaking and practical learning activities and a very safe, supportive learning environment. As a student, you feel pushed to learn and try out new competencies. Manner of teaching is so wonderful and refreshing!! She's patient and supportive but knows how to motivate her students. She's great at building confidence and keeping lessons fun and engaging through a variety of activities that improve conversation, writing, and reading skills

♡ I marked your word ma'am (" If you want to achieve greatness stop asking for permission.") 🔥 💯

– Arbaaz

I have 3 years of experience in a different field but I was not happy still with what I was doing as I was confused. So, after research, I luckily got Mrs. Monika, Ebullient Career Counsellor & Life coach. She did my pre-counseling in detail. She is so friendly that she not only gives you the best career advice, also if u will share your problems she will give the best advice ever for this and you will feel relieved and motivated. Then she provided me with a career assessment test and after a detailed study of that test, she gave me better insight into my personality and my best-ever career options based on my personality. I am feeling now more confident about my career and I am heading towards my goal with more energy and clarity. So, at any stage of life if someone is confused and feeling down then she is the best person whom u can contact at any time. And I am lucky I contacted her. A special thanks to Mrs. Monika for providing me with better insight about myself and I got a great friend, mentor, and counsellor in life.......

– Mohit Gill (New Delhi)

She is an amazing person with an awe-inspiring personality The way she talks and the way she explains things with real-life examples is just mesmerizing She offers you genuine advice and does not only go on promoting her company like others, she just wants the best of the students and explains the need of counselling for every student. She is very Frank, cordial and student-friendly I don't really have words to explain her amazing character I would highly recommend her Rating:10/5 I would be amazing if u book a pre counselling session with her

– Amanpreet Kaur Arza

Ms.Monica is an efficient and skillful professional. A good counselor has flexibility in world views and a strong understanding capability... Being able to communicate when things aren't working, and then offering to refer the client to another professional who may be able to better aid them is one hallmark of a good counselor. She helps in understanding one's self and realizing our abilities. She is such a friendly and positive person who has helped me and guided me to decide on which institute to choose for a particular course. She is a highly patient listener and has an understanding personality. I highly recommend her counseling services. Do visit or meet her at least once to choose your career path or be it for higher studies. She would be the right person to guide you. The epitome of a counsellor.

– Syed Khajaji (Bangalore)

EPILOGUE

These were the 7 SECRETS NOBODY TOLD YOU EVER TO BUILD A SUCCESSFUL CAREER. By applying these secrets one can build a successful career. As I did for myself & for my clients. People who apply these new learnings will get a bonus. They will not only build a successful career but transform their life too.

SUMMARY

In the book, the author took the most burning question of the audience which is "how to build a successful career". She spoke about the 7 secrets, starting from setting a definite goal (master key to success). Second, breaking out of conformity, which is what most of us were lacking. Third, to achieve anything in life, we need to be perseverant. Fourth, accept our failure & treat it as a stepping stone in our career. Fifth, worry brings fear hence we need to stop it & start living. Sixth, she discussed, which is faced by almost every one of us that is mobile addiction & how to reduce it. Lastly, she emphasized the importance of asking for help from the right person & importance of having a career coach to build a successful career in a short time.

ACKNOWLEDGEMENT

I would like to sincerely thank the following people for their valuable support for me, which has helped me in writing this book & become an excellent coach.

*Inspiring Jatin (Author Mentor): The real motivation behind writing this book (it was a dream for years).

*Master My Life Community (ICF Coaching)

*Mrs.Monisha Advani: - My life's second-inning mentor- Mam is always there to guide me in the right way, throughout my journey.

*Mr.NK.Subbiah (My Brother):- He is my all-time mentor since childhood.

*Edumilestones:- Supported me to figure out my counseling passion & take it as a career.

* Shreans Daga Foundation - Thanks to the 28 days spiritual journey, which actually shaped my life.

*Mr.Dev Gadhvi (Passionpreneur community):- The turning point of my life, i.e., investment in self-development started during the passionpreneur summit

Acknowledgement

*Iron Lady Program by Mr.Rajesh Bhat – My first transformational program. Finding the Real Me

*Mrs.Deepakumari (Manager Randstad – Hosur)- My Guru, who taught me in & out about Human Resources.

*My lovely Kids- V.Meenakshi & V.Kris Palaniappan for their love & valuable support.

*My wonderful family, who always believed in me.

www.ingramcontent.com/pod-product-compliance
Lightning Source LLC
LaVergne TN
LVHW041545070526
838199LV00046B/1830